EINSTEIN'S CAT

Books by Zoë Landale

Blue in This Country
Burning Stone
Colour of Winter Air
Einstein's Cat
Harvest of Salmon: Adventures in Fishing the BC Coast
Once a Murderer
Slice me some truth: An anthology of Canadian creative nonfiction (Co-editor)
The Rain is Full of Ghosts

EINSTEIN'S CAT

poems

ZOË LANDALE

WOLSAK
& WYNN

Cover art and design: Leigh Kotsilidis
Author's photograph: Cathryn Lawrence
Typset in Garamond & Warnok Pro
Printed by Coach House Printing Company Toronto, Canada

The publisher gratefully acknowledges the support of the Canada Council for the Arts, the Ontario Arts Council and the Canada Book Fund.

Wolsak and Wynn Publishers Ltd.
280 James Street North
Hamilton, ON
Canada L8R 2L3

Library and Archives Canada Cataloguing in Publication

Landale, Zoë, 1952-
    Einstein's cat / Zoë Landale.

Poems.
ISBN 978-1-894987-67-7

    I. Title.

PS8573.A5315E55 2012   C811'.54   C2012-904740-6

Home is a name, a word, it is a strong one; stronger than magician ever spoke, or spirit ever answered to, in the strongest conjuration.
Charles Dickens

Home is so sad. It stays as it was left,
shaped to the comfort of the last to go
as if to win them back.
Philip Larkin

CONTENTS

3   Where is the calliope music? Where is home?

Say, what genre is this universe playing in, anyway?

high definition, if we let it

Second star to the right and straight on till morning.
J. M. Barry

LETHE

[Director's cut]

The universe's genre is noir,
thanks for asking

This is the melancholy season of sky
where all we thought we'd ever learned
leaches and pales to leaf skeletons.
The dead nourish us.
We trudge on, unmindful of their roots,

earned
patience rolled grey,
a sheet of lead

how the white threading
of their love still sustains us

sodden ground.
There was music once, and bright paint;

we wore sky like a larger coat

the harsh coats of dogs
smelled of wood smoke,
the cold freshness of stars.

In warm houses we stand, noses
to misty glass, breathe in
the daily forgetfulness that brought us here.
Some days the rain is horizontal; others, vertical,
whispering lines that blur memory.

orphan: the last one standing,
toes curled
over the drop-off of dark

This is the season of mountains saturated:
the snowline comes lower
every week.
Salmon streams are high
with blackened carcasses, the rush
and runnel of water.

ache of lost home, lights on
gleaming wood

It's hope we've lost,
a wondrous feather, blue
suffused with gold, the length of a woman's
forearm, something we found and swore
to keep forever, but we laid it down
at the edge of a field,
only we've forgotten what field,
on the edge of what river,   [the Tsolum river]
flowing clear and hurriedly over rocks
and sand.

Beside the feather,
we recall shapes the current made;
indented jade arabesques.
All the rest gone –
drums, the particular milky-green grace of oats
against sky –
lost in the mantra our eyes make circling
wind-rumpled ovoids
on water that promises   over here –
                                                              we're waiting

        and promises revelation.

still life: bedroom with dvd

in the movie, a messenger arrives at the castle, panting   the hero's father
is dead   the hero, nostrils wide with testosterone, wheels through the
great hall doorway, the diva flashes after

in the bedroom, two watchers: the man notices the diva's breasts, the
woman thinks *nice dress*, medieval sleeves a swish of red wings

the watchers loll against the bright darks of an Amish quilt (black, rose,
indigo) so new the woman shivers with pride as she strokes it

the man likes the Irish wolfhound in the movie, which pretends sleep, but
a brown eye slit fixes on the roast pig close to the table's edge   the dog's
ear large as a farmwife's hand twitches

        umm, can we pause? the woman asks

the man fumbles for the remote   listens to water sounds from the
bathroom   sigh   he's in this for the long howl

thinks, no matter what latitude and longitude he find himself in, *there*
becomes *here*, that pivotal axis, the right now, the planet's roads and air
routes fling out from him in long brilliant arms like sunstars   wherever
he is, or travels to, or the woman, or the luscious diva, each one becomes
the centre of the world, the hub

flopped out on the quilt, everything: clouds, global warming, eBay, the
fireplace he wants in the kitchen, all revolve around him, the centre

wow

what star power

CANDLES FOR YOUR FATHER

When your father died   even now, heartstrings go
                                                   sprrung
you were driving past yellow alder trees
to the store for milk;
life's urgencies zooming on, vivid, a roller coaster,
stomach hurtling out through your mouth
like a starfish
with the motion of his death.

You hate roller coasters.

Death is a shade
of mother of pearl.   a pale bird whistles up your breath

You knew he was going.
The phone lines were wool crossed over
a woman's hands as she winds them
into skeins: news from the hospital.
Your sister asked for prayer
solid enough to lean on.   between gold & the lustre
                                                   of swan feathers

Tonight, she said, three
thousand miles
                          away.
It was Friday, twilight misty
as you plummeted down Ryan hill
to the store.
In your head,
you wrote a letter, told him maple leaves
had finally achieved fall, gone
from half-yellow to red
as insistent as bells
while scarlet ninebark bushes lined the road.
                                      starlets, triumphant

In the valley, lights blossomed
into blue-white bouquets
in the approaching dark;
everyone was coming home.   going

Sprightly and joyful,
a hymn ambushed you
and you thought *What's this*,
not sure it was right to sing when he was dying
and you wished him ease and were crying
because you couldn't bear the thought
of no more cards in the mail.

                              hit the doornail, talk to you
                              of love, you'll show us
                              boxes of his blue writing

But you sang because it's what you were given,
gave thanks that you were given anything
though the leaves had turned, finally,
and in another five minutes
you would come out of the store,
swinging a gallon of milk.

                              cold leaking through skin

        You found out later your father died then.

                              for him, a quick slip into the open
                              a creak of oars

On the way up the hill, you stopped singing but
in the car, the tune still pulsed
as though the air
was scored with quick musical joy.

At home, your daughter, a dog and a cat
waited, every light switched on.
You were desperate to return
to gold radiance from windows, falling
oblong on the walk,
worried now that you'd left

every candle you owned burning;
beacons to light your father, however short
a way,
on the path he went alone.

                                    ferryman's eyes reflect
                                              sparks

WAKE WITH CANDLES

On the front porch, a neighbour tied
a black cloth bow around a pillar;
the sight of it
made you gasp.   how many *hundreds* of years?
The bow's ritual satin   it isn't just in books
called up unease like wings.
You ricocheted between scarlet roses,
smokers, those in the living room
dry with grief.

You remembered your father
with all the candles
even he could have wished.   flame as radiance, naked
                                                 as a hand

Dozens of red glass votives,
their message of yearning
burned all over his dimmed house.

Darkness, flowers and flame.   natural habitat of shadows
Ruby prayers.

Down in the unfinished basement,
others were saying cigarette prayers   damaged

enough to make the eyes water,
yet you kept crowding in with them
on bare wooden stairs
where he had sat and smoked
until the years, beads of water,
ran into one another,
puddled.   & were gone

The stairs as close to him as you could get,
then.
On the concrete wall
his youngest daughter drew a heart
with his name and dates inside.
Your private wailing wall, though
No one cried,
then.

loss squats on the chest
with cold avian feet
& stomps

You remembered your father with the candles
he loved.
In the dark dining room, you laid out

fire & chrysanthemums burning
like bronze, the melt of autumn

meat, cheese, bread, fruit,
patisserie cakes, heraldic
with curls of chocolate,
a spread you swooped on, hungry
after days of no meals.

who would have thought there
could be so much to arrange?

Still, you could not eat much,
busy keeping the dead nearby
with *Remember when?*
You warmed yourself, held tears at bay
with your intense communion
of candles.

the oldest story: bright
against night

YOUR FATHER'S GHOST

Two weeks after your father's death,   winter light slides thin
                                                  as wind
you watch motion reflect
from lit kitchen windows.
You knead bread, watch him outside.
Only when you look sideways do you see
him move quickly –
this after four years of only the most
careful easings from chair to stairs,
slowly out to the Royal Oak pub for coffee.
Never breath enough.

Age spots on your father's
high forehead fade,
wrinkles smooth. He is a man younger
than when you were born;
someone you know only from old photographs.
All that's familiar
is the humour and the eyes.   blue flash
The grass is long; you can't make out the time
of year where he walks but
there's a luxe
to the way he strides;
he leans into motion   devotion, that sand cliff, runnel
                                     of grains as you climb

the way a man with unlimited
money   spends.

He is foreshortened,
a figure bounding away from all of you,
and it's not that he is neglectful   can't hear
but even as you don't think
about albacore with their wise black eyes
schooling off Mexico,
he does not think about family.
At some point he will remember   affection reliable
                                      as breath

but right now this journey is the whole of him,
there's a raptness one sees in animals,
a delighted concentration;
the retriever streaks after its yellow tennis ball,
a black kitten pats a twist of foil.   it's called narrow field of vision

Now it's midmorning, but outside
is underwater dark.   sudden grey breath of coming rain
November wind is rising.
In the kitchen, you cover the loaves
with a red-and-white towel.
Outside, Siberian iris expire
in dramatic heaps of foliage,
yellow-striped along spiky edges.
In life, your family is flamboyant, loyal,
and often despairs.
Now, your father's ghost   weightless as abstraction
(in the glass you watch closely)

            slides away from the iris,
            away from you
            utterly concentrated.

MOON DOG, HURRYING

Christmas rests upon the mountains,
approaches blue-perfect as sky   make it right, make-believe
and gleams of sun from the glacier.
Expensive strawberries
for your daughter's birthday
insert a fragrance intoxicating as high summer;
a burst of present-tense fruit,
sweet and seedy on the tongue.

                                                  come splashed on
                                                  your breasts

The day is a medieval tapestry.   you are angry
                                                  wool and shadows

Old, rich colours, heavy
maroons and blacks.

As you move,
the mountains rush beside you,
like when you were a kid
travelling in the car
and the moon came with you   a glowing dog
following every time you glanced out
the window, though sometimes
it still surprises you
by nosing around the other side.

Today the swoosh and blink of air
is not a moon dog hurrying,
but death.
Your father, gone five weeks now,
gestures, your mother waves
from both sides of the divide,
weighing less now than your thin daughter,
newly fourteen.

Two days ago in sleep, your mother said
this was her last Christmas;
your husband awoke and asked why
you were crying; you said it had that   forsaken
ache and snap of true revelation.   the raven that followed you
                                                       for months carrying its gold
                                                       chain of unseemly desire
                                                       for another man,
                                                       vanished to the blue
                                                       mountains

Meanwhile, you mail presents;
she is still here there is just
less and less of her.
Your hound snouts your hand;
for her the day is full.
Smells and motion through the forest
are enough, and pats.

While your family jitters on the cusp
(brown-velvet mysteries of departure)   thin icy pain
you would be a fire burning
on the near shore of a moonlit river,
steady
despite the wind that wants   farther in and higher up
to lure us all

                 to transformation.   the glacier's sweet white

meantime, behind the screen

away from the white blinding [spellbinding] arc lights, the director has a
hissy fit on his cellphone   the diva and the hero lounge in folding chairs
so turquoise they almost fluoresce
the back of each chair inscribed

death makes me hungry, the diva says   a bowl of popcorn the size of a
pumpkin balances on a chair arm between her and the hero

catch, says the hero

SNAP go wolfhound jaws   the grey dog's head level with theirs, white
reflects on the creature's eyes from lights one set away

SNAP – [insert the sound at five second intervals for the rest of the
scene]
the hero eats one kernel, tosses one

the dog looks so intelligent when there's food, the diva says   *I hope this is light
popcorn, I did ask for light*

the hero is cynical, of course, it's in his job description, along with tall
dark and the h-word   *don't think so   the dog wouldn't eat it otherwise*   [in
real life, the hero's father is alive and fly-fishing in Wisconsin]
he goes back to the diva's remark about their scene: *know what the Harry
Potter books say about death?*

the diva shakes her head, doesn't like any fantasy but her own, buff and
prancing

"To the well-organised mind, death is but the next great adventure."

well I hope my next adventure is one without a hound of the Baskervilles guest
starring, the diva says, snappish herself at the repeated *clop* of giant jaws

the director stomps back, glowers at the munching trio: *let's get a move on*

FACE DOWN IN A FIELD OF STARS

Outside your window, white bleeding hearts
bloom beside the stream bed, dry.   bells with no clappers
Earth lies pale, parched
You'll go no more a-roving
to the market.
                                       jauntiness, around your shoulders,
                                       a red-striped scarf

You learnt a whole park by heart
to tell your father its secrets:
the gloss and prickle of Oregon grape, brown fur
on sword ferns' unfolding tips.
All the lips of green.
                                       at any moment, leaves
                                       will open, he will burst through
                                       into some vast understanding
                                       a hallway where he stands
                                       by the pillars, bewildered

He died before you could share them.
Now he's off gadding,
Cassiopeia, the Pleiades cluster spread
all the lustrous tricks of light
before his fascinated sight,
and him without a camera.
He's gone where no letters can find him.
                                       understanding: another name
                                       for *yield*

There are no fish in streams there.
Gases flow in hot arcs; you don't have names
for the rosy explosions of fusion.
He used to grow yellow begonias
in pots outside his door.
You've asked but he has not told you
if there are flowers.
The ragged dangle that is your life dismays you;
sprays of bleeding heart holding aloft
tiny white griefs.

You want to live alone, a sunflower
in some radiant kingdom,
to stop being
phototropic,
turning to the warmth
in men's eyes.

in the great hall, squinting
in the luminosity pouring down
from high windows, can he tell
you how?

What he shows in reply:
your body planted face down
in a field of stars,   like lying on hot daisies
the whistling of light
a wind through your stubborn bones.

MILKY WAY

Night. Stars come home
and nest, lamps come to sudden rest upon
the dark doorways of cottages
beside the sea.

                    roosting firebirds with
                    tails of bright

Lights, comforting as seraphs,
hold back the black that rises from land
as wisps
as memory.

                    we walk swirled
                    by the gauzy past

Sea breathes the smell of shells
and bladderwrack;
houses trail out supper into the night,
the lemony scent of soap.

Doors are bulwarks,
the square-shouldered
back of them shut
against dusk.

                    we are outside
                    for the ride,
                    for eternity

Stars are confetti, luminous
welcoming the stealing dark
above damp meadows.
Rising like ground mist
languor of tiredness; sweet
letting go.

                    pop of transition between
                    consciousness and un-, a pearl
                    felt in the dark

The cold fire of starlight, golden spangles
of lamplight, these are
dangles we hold up,
guardians, and watch

                    from the train

and drop   when we are ready.
Tugging of eyelids
down.
Grace of place;
the watching, invisible stars.

STAR BLOOD

I will love the light for it shows me the way,
yet I will endure the darkness for it shows me the stars.
                    Og Mandino

The magenta stuff in the photograph
is star blood, ten thousand years old   *displacement activity:*
and wisped about most satisfactorily,   home a puckered wound
                                                  that won't stand weight

a ghost blown
on the high winds of heaven out
in luminous streamers
                    into black gulfs
                              between living stars.

Blue and white signatures seraphic
in intensity.   make me a saint but not just yet,
                                                  as St. A said

The long-gone star a colossal gas body,
not haze,
but rosy   attenuated streaks,
as though particles of exploded sun
clung together in a parody
of good cheer, bands reluctant to part
with companions they once burned with
so fiercely.

Dispersing, the star achieves
immensity enough
to wrap whole light years of the Milky Way
with trailers of slowly expanding pink
raising death
            to
                  translucent
                        artifice.   device, our own Earth sexual as a lily
                                     bloom & glorious

STAR CHARTS

How alluring the dots in a star atlas,   glorious compass, the night sky
orange and green with spider legs marking variable
stars or open clusters.   Doppler, the red
                                                 cry of lives slamming sideways

The radiating sky cut by lines, an infinite pie:
Phoenix, Hydrus, Chamaeleon.
Arbitrary, the wedges of star fields
must seem to the acolyte –
still the names beckon: afternoon in Eridanus,
could worlds exist there, a light-breeze ocean
fit for the slipstream of a tiny sailboat   devote yourself to the sane untying
                                                  of imagination

in blue July?

Always we see ourselves in the boat
with sunburnt arms and face,
a glass of lemonade in hand, so cold,
condensation   beads.   feeds our desire for surcease
                                                  from garishly hued drama

We are eager for stars of fresh colours,
horizons we could never have imagined,
ready for adventure
or brisk stellar winds, whichever
comes first.

It is tempting to think of space flat as a map;
stars as islands with a backdrop of pale blue,
white shallows of hot Carina and Crux
like reefs in the Gulf of Georgia.
But space pushes out in all directions

including time,
green wake a-froth with bubbles.

We must redesign the boat,
become ourselves, fish inside looking out, adept

accept the slush & flush
of *Mare Tranquillitatis*

at negotiating black, the bursts of chroma
the atlas insists are there in stars
our eyes barely seem to see.

wobbly

[in actual fact the Sea of
Tranquility is a dry punched-
out crater on the Moon; or,
alternate entry: *he used a blow
torch to create the iridescence on the
carbon-steel wings*]

We could cultivate twilight vision,
the Purkinje effect: reds darken,
we decipher blues and greens as lighter
than by day.

The portholes fill.
We swim.
Enclosed, we evade jewelled dimensions

pummelled but outright thrilled
to be flying

of light.

Watching ghosts: luminous, tropical, hurtling

you have the best seat in the house

Ghosts, we hope, may be always with us...
Elizabeth Bowen

Einstein's cat

in the bedroom, the watchers link hands on top of the rosy-violet-night
splendour of their new quilt   the castle in the movie looks like the last
words in drafts, the woman thinks, all that stone, *brrr*, it'd be cold in
winter   the man understands now why his brother-in-law told him to see
this movie, the diva is well, what a woman, juicy, Spanish, enough to
reduce even a thinking kind of guy to a mass of boiling roiling hormones
    the watchers snuggle closer, give off an *afterward* vibe

    ring ring

the screen-dream shatters like raku in an earthquake   *oo*, they're in the
dark and where's the phone?   it's painful brushing off all these sharp
shards of fantasy

pause it, will you? the woman says, which the man does when she finds the
light switch

the man answers, doesn't give the phone over   it isn't their child or a
long lost friend and judging from the level of drama in his voice
(apparently three out of a possible ten), no one they know has died or
been injured

the woman recalls hearing Albert Einstein talk about radio

> *"You see, wire telegraph is a kind of a very, very long cat. You pull his tail in
> New York and his head is meowing in Los Angeles. Do you understand
> this? And radio operates exactly the same way: you send signals here, they
> receive them there. The only difference is that there is no cat."*

the woman thinks *hmm*, what enormous ghost cat are we allowing into the
house?

At Some Level of the Universe

All dimensions are critical dimensions,
otherwise why are they there?
        Russ Zandbergen

At some level of the universe
she is always
ten, mother and daughter stepping
toward the stairs   put on airs, the Ritz
arms around each other
in a locked walk
that is a jokey hug;
the mom touching the girl's tummy,
saying *I'm so fat all of a sudden*,
while the child giggles,
steers her toward her black cat
for one last pat.   combat of *being there* with awareness,
                            the stop sign that could pop them out

Somewhere   of the lit house with fir windows
the child will always echo
her mother as they climb
the stairs to bed,
chant *I'm Jocelyn Elizabeth bean-child*,
though she is also the kid who wants
to dye her hair red,
to have cool clothes,
a girl capable of terrifying sarcasm.
She would scream if her friends
could hear her now:
I'm Jocelyn Elizabeth bean-child.   laughter plush, an amber Zeppelin
                            to bump against

The mother marvels
how the parent's joy in the girl repeats
in her voice.
That affection lights her
into the night
of her bedroom,
alone with guinea pig, hamster
and thirty stuffed animals.

crescent moon a fable, rising
behind two firs

Singing, she enters her kingdom.

POLARIS

Your daughter found Polaris the other night,
out her window in the sky beyond
the Douglas firs. *My first constellation,*   consternation
she kept saying, as if recognition were a lustrous
thing, remarkable in its sudden condensation.   intervene, astonishment:
                                                                          the country night sky
                                                                          is mystery ablaze

Now she wants a telescope
and the starry January sky
is a mystical whirl of shapes
with lit innards that pass by her room
every evening after dinner,
a celestial join-the-dots to find the figure.

The North Star is a marker for escaped slaves:
a dreamy luminosity for your daughter to hang
reveries on.   She is reading about
a black woman who escaped to Canada –
the child sees herself as
The True North Strong and Free,
and cheers Polaris on:
good work.   quirk of these immense
                                                                          star clusters
                                                                          suddenly seen –
                                                                          where were they before?

Obedient star.   Lawful star, lighting the way
across borders and through glass, luring
an eleven-year-old heart who has never been
lost in a dark country beyond all protection.
Though she tries hard to imagine the alien
hemlock and alder swamps lit by the Big Dipper,
the moon,   night noises.
Only last week she saw a yellow
stalking-cat sign on a store door:
Cougar Alert.
Four minutes from home.   big cats   roam

Though your daughter tries to stay with Polaris,
her imagination betrays her.   refers to the tangible: fleece, fur
Dark earth draws her back
to the escaped slave, the cougar
who wisps above the crisp ground
silent as mist
with paws that drive hexagonal frost crystals
an inch down into the path.

                                                see tracks a mile from home

She asks again for a telescope,
wants to fall through her eyes
into that strange void of luminosities
in the sky
with no more distractions.   attraction reaction, the abstract
                                                an abrupt polished-copper pull

Let the Archer, the Scorpion tell her
their stories of light.   she'll slide up to meet them

watching from the centre

on the bed, the man thumbs the remote to restart the movie   [the woman has not told him quite how much the genuine Amish quilt cost]

the two of them don't know that to the bright figures onscreen, they are the blur of backlit heads, the man still thinks he's pivoting from the centre of the world [shamans call this from the middle of the tent *"I am at the centre of the world,"* and then away they climb to the spirit realm]

but he does wonder, only if we're *all* at the centre, then who's not?

in the movie, the plot moves on with many a hitch   the man is mesmerized by the diva's tits like watermelons bobbing in water, not green and stripey, of course, just pink life preservers hanging down her front

onscreen the hero pretends not to be riveted but the man notices he licks his lips more than the narrative warrants   the woman thinks the hero's the medieval equivalent of the Marlboro Man, a manly man, not much up top, but hotter than a fireplace in the kitchen

MARCH IS A LIT MONTH

First-born among flowering shrubs,
Indian plum blooms, its tiny white prayers, crinkly
as sprigged muslin,

nostalgia zips red as a
ruby throat;
swing against dark bark.
you embark on the litany
once a upon a time

March is a lit month
in the soaked woods' chapel.

You need these prayers. You need
circles of intercession, rising:
hope deferred makes the whole heart sick.

You put the marsh in context:
a habitat that breathes like you but slower,
a wet-mud maritime, its water swells and lowers
the balsam exhale of cottonwood
it's understood how this soothes
exuberant as a red balloon
ribbon wound about a child's wrist.

persistence of obsession
you pull an aromatic leaf
toward you
like a rose

March is a hard month to walk around in.
On river paths you clatter like a dried
pea inside a maraca;
battered by *shake-a shake-a boom*
your dead seem more well-disposed than the living.

In the bush, frogs have not yet begun

while you are corduroy,
brown & undone
When the desire comes, it is a tree of life –
green hallelujahs.

April Ghosts

April is a rueful season for ghosts.   makes the most of the little
                                                        they are

Strengthening light attenuates them
to gossamer   pulled apart, bright,
thready as thistledown.   overhead fluff

It hurts the woman that she laughs but she does.
Death just keeps calling ghosts back,
stretching them into luminous handfuls
All they say is *white*.   in spite of themselves

What kind of answer is that?   polite? contrite?

Does it fertilize the fields?
Does the coarse bristle of meadow grass
grow juicier, do the thoroughbreds in their blankets

understand the universe better for *white*?
What's out there beyond the oval
mouth of light
that swallowed our ghosts and where
do they come back from to pluck at us?   finesse a long wooden stirring
                                                        stick from this blurred,
                                                        wrenching
                                                        dimension

Does it smell like cinnamon? Dust?
Do trees lean black against the horizon at dusk,
like here? Is there something graceful we're supposed to do
in response to haunting – offer chocolate or joss sticks,

some kind of white thought?
Is there something we're supposed to see
through, like this muddy world with its homicides
and sudden acts of sweetness?   complete uncolour, shining
                                                        like mist

This is a brutal month for ghosts.
They can't make themselves understood;
against April-blue sky the woman watches
them drop
                like shot birds.

BLUE ONE IN THE SURF LINE

An angel flies overhead, one of the blue
ones.　　　　Your dog tenses at the hiss
of feathers.　　　　It lands　　　　you'd never call one silent
at the bright wet
edge between ocean and rock.
The dog quivers, head to one side,
undecided whether to chase.

June, and the year rolls over green
and sunny.　　You perch
on a boulder, stroke
the dog who adores you,
watch the angel who also represents　　descent
affection or at least something glittering

　　　　　　　　　　　　　　　　tactility of love:
　　　　　　　　　　　　　　　　a woman braids a five-year-
　　　　　　　　　　　　　　　　old's hair

or it would not be here
on the wind-scoured beach.

A moment before, your thoughts
splintered like a broken chickadee leg,
and the dog came　　　and leaned on you.
That was one answer.
The angel is another, though
it brings only assurance　　　chance
　　　　　　　　　　　　　　red coat of belonging, warm
that the spent and fragrant　　over the shoulders
pods from the cottonwoods count
as humus or a blessing.
Meanwhile, there is cold in the wind.
The dog judges the angel
is too far to catch, nudges *let's go.*

This blue one stands in the surf line　　fine
All the brilliant day swirls about it
in an easing *hissh.*

44

BABY STARS: SOUTH PENDER ISLAND

Sun braids strips of light
along a tide line.   intertwine of consciousness
                                                watching with the body radiant
                                                as a well-run dog

Summer is high and blue
illumined by guardian spirits,
bull kelp, its slow brown transfigured
to a white neck of light, floating.   remote, isolate

Out toward the islands
busy sailboats pull sound
behind them, masts bare
in their lilting horizontal of water.
The blue pause of mountains in sun.

On shore three children
move in murmurous bubbles
intent on rocks, shells and baby starfish.   wishes in red, blue, green, purple
Baby stars, they call them.

Sea lettuce glistens at their feet;
its open skin
sheets of green vowels that taste of salt.

Higher up, a woman picks popping wrack,
there's the gift of grit attached
to living tissue and clattering.

A spirit rattle
wet   in the hand.   demand
                                                to be used

Home Again, She Wonders Why the Language of Comfort has Dried into Stains Like Squashed Blackberries

In a swept kitchen, a man embraces a woman
who endures his touch
sullen as an onion.
She could be on the other side of an island
one of those half-acre ones
that crowd the coast like clouds,
rock and fir and moss underfoot, so dry
it crunches.   she will not cry

Five minutes ago she was fertilizing,   portrait:
                                                                                    Self-soothing in Garden

wondering if her bones
would look like the powdered lumps
she was spreading when the crematorium
finished with her.   pardon?
She was happy, comparatively speaking.

                                                                                    freaking morbid, if
                                                                                    you ask me

When she came into the kitchen
her husband told her one of his two
blood relatives   hates her.

                                                                                    concentrate

No wonder she doesn't respond to his hugs.
Now, standing with his arms in a ring
around her that brings no ease,
he tells her bone meal is no kind of answer.

She is desperate as a girl at the bottom of a pool
desperate for air, to emerge into light.
Really, she'd like to be convinced,   of brightness
have him stroke her hair.
If only she could believe

in something shining   hard enough,
from the other side of the island,
she could turn
inside his arms, she could hug him back.   the black tide would subside

If only his body spoke
the language of comfort it used to,

she could breathe.

When He Left, the Air Smelled like Cold Water and Stone

When he left on Friday night
she felt like a blank sheet
of paper when the pen about to write on it
is laid down again by someone: all white.   spite sizzling like hot fat

When he left she felt thin
as the words *I'm sorry*
left unsaid;
the way they hang echoing
in an ill-lit hallway with brown carpet,
a hotel everyone else has abandoned.   the tandem yells they do
                                               to a farewell

When he left she waited for him
to come back.
He did, twice that night,
for things he had forgotten:
his shaving kit, to drop off dirty laundry
in a green plastic garbage bag
and tell her he'd be back for it.
At length there was only night, echoing.
          The golden dog beside her bed.
No more slam of doors.   a crow hit
                                by a car; fluids & bones glint
                                in all the wrong places

When he left, she slept
as if plummeting into a well.
There was a familiar smell of cold water
and stone.
               She
                    fell
                         for hours, hugging herself.

Darkness wore on. She remembered the cranberry scones
he cooked each Saturday morning,
thought, *What can we possibly
now have for breakfast?*

48

SCARLET FLAG

When he left her
and returned   before six the next morning,
she was not surprised.
He hadn't needed his shaving kit after all.
She put on her dressing gown
did laundry as if

> what if one them died?
> coping thought #38: ~~bad~~

the swish and smell of soap
could slacken the strain

on trust, how the fabric of their years
was pulling apart
with logarithmic acceleration:
his accusations, the resentment

> presentiment, DING,
> you're wrong

a kite she insisted
on flying in storm-force winds.

> ears pinned back
> to the fight before

She was reinventing herself, she was training
to be a scarlet flag any place other than here.
Eyes closed, face fixed

in lines of exhaustion, he recited again
the litany of how she crackled in gales.
Change was necessary, but not
this change. Not this red, fabric, nor time.

> change = crime

She said *I'm sorry,* went back to bed
tired of falling into limp folds
each time he entered the house
angry, always angry.
Why was she doing this?
Because being a flag was something she wanted:
that simple, that unacceptable.

> crime = ballistic

When he came back
to the bedroom, she flapped
a question at him
the size and scratchiness of a wool blanket:
Do you realize what your absence all night
has ripped?

wrong = strong in the wrong
direction

TRUST AND POPPIES

What he asks is too hard:
to make the long brown stems of their marriage
break green again.   give up *disdain?*

No one resurrects poppies in the fall.
Today the woman pulled armloads of them
by the stream, crisp as kindling.   light dwindles like hay
                                                    that's been rained on

What flame she has is drawn back
far to a bay north of here, where ocean
licks the sky all the way to Japan.

Such deep wet kisses.

Melancholy streaks of extinguishing light,
sparks floating out to sea.
Moan of a whistle buoy.   the iron in her life
                                                    floated then,
                                                    she hugged metal; it cut
All the red she owns exists in memory.
Raspberry-hued day lilies, roses the shade of claret;
on the beach she had only the flicker
of it behind her eyes,

the transitory grace of fire.
She thought of him then, the moonlight fitful.
In the tent, the girls like puppies

shook the nylon and whispered secrets
in voices too close to the language
of blowing mist to be coincidence.   dance of false signals

White sand, fire, the curling glyphs
of waves. Pewter giving way to silver.
Poppy heads with their hoards of seed.

It is autumn now and what he asks
with his husband's hands, his careful touch,   much too little
is more than any gardener can promise.

Even among shrubs, only box and yew
break reliably from old wood.
Once an annual is finished, all a person can do   accrue yearning for return
of bloom

is hope for the unpredictable flare of germination.

HARD IN THE HAND

She never told lies to sticks.
Hard in the hand, they were what
she wanted and threw far out in the swamp
where water lilies bloomed
yellow, each with a single penile stamen.

      heretic, inflexible

      fixation, cayenne in a cut

What's the point in disguising
the truth from wood? Cast your complaint
on the waters and it will come back to you
wet, in the mouth of a dog
who understands anxiety like a musician;
all the pluckings of gut that give glissando,
crescendo, diminuendo.

      [got the cringing down pat]

She has been ready to receive truth
from stars, trees, whatever
was at hand and in a wisdom-dispensing
mode.   All it takes is an open
intercession – why not, you've lost
all the furniture that was once so
nicely arranged – and the most
peaceful of lives becomes
loquacious.   *Ask and you shall receive*
from the night sky, swamp cedars,
even those with no legs.

      through the facade, golden-rod

      the task a slug takes on
      is to glorify eternity in slime

A stick, too, is its own form
of conversation
that *zing* of weight so satisfying
as it leaves the hand –

      banzai!

OCTOBER STORM

When she gets up in the morning

she is going to leave him.
The day is grey,
drags her along
lines of dust on the floor.
The sky streaks of cold October rain.
Storm warning for the north coast,
the radio says.

When she gets up, she has been wrestling
with demons, dreams all night
and a wakeful cat.
She is a hundred feet long,
a quarter inch thick.
Outside the bedroom window,
maple leaves startle, amber
blowing stars with red handles
that flip in the rising wind.

She sweeps the floor,
makes lunch for her daughter
who is perfectly able to make her own,
but it pleases them to exchange
this flourish of tangible affection.
The girl will miss her father.

In the woman's mind, he is a muddle
of broken boards open
to weather.
When she gets up, he is a dock,
she walks on him.
By noon, though, through some sleight
she doesn't understand,
he is grey, but full form.

anger a hard blue ball,
bounces in a wood-floored gym

strong gusts

shorn of civility

diphthong, a scarlet ribbon

shocks
phenomena of moving light

smell of sawdust
farther away

silver

grand ground if you can stand i⸝

54

In rain-streaked glass she sees his reflection
cooking Sunday supper;
lights on in the kitchen, radio playing.

The sizzle and delicious smell as garlic and ginger hit
a hot pan.

The storm is upon them.   Outside,

atmosphere a tarpaulin, torn,
flapping with turbulence

fir branches break, skitter
along green in horizontal rain.
The clamour of swift-rushing air.

As she watches his ghost
in the rain,

summary pain as the heart
reorients

she cannot remember why
she saw him as less
than three-dimensional.
For the first time, she understands
she probably can't leave him.
Almost twenty years together
they fight and flip like leaves
in the wind, fall
face-together again.

Is it loyalty, thick as a ship hawser?   answer!
Food prepared for one another,
lovingly and with clean napkins?
The wood and shine of their house?
All these woven seamlessly with
the pounce of a fat cat
on a toe,
a daughter so tall now she leans
an elbow on her mother's shoulder?

When the woman got up in the morning
she knew everything bad there was to know
about their life together;
by noon she is amnesiac
and grateful.   She thinks.   white instinct kinked like
                                                         a root

collision of the worlds, much noise, a twilight, H. G. Wells lowering sky

the dark-haired diva escapes from the DVD into the watchers' garden where three vulva-coloured Stargazer lilies have opened two almost-open trumpets have the pursed lips of a hero about to whistle   curled back petals and orange-tipped stamens exult in a silent sexual carnival; how in the world, the diva wonders, did lilies get chosen to be the funeral flower?   only those would have been white Madonnas, domesticated for 1,500 years, since Minoan times purity, and all that, good enough for the bees [poor drones, the workers chop off their wings in fall, push them out of the hive while they try to cling on with their feet]

this solo au naturel *wasn't my idea*, the diva says, looking directly at the watchers, breaking John Gardiner's number one rule about *fictional dream* and *suspension of disbelief*   she rubs her nose crossly   *divas belong on sets or stages with a glorious amount of makeup and sizable penile adulation   we don't like dinky backyards, or high wires   these are settings for the hero, only he's done a runner, as my English pal says, when planning to leave with his bills unpaid*

her(o) the

her being the   working syllable in this episode [note the earlier association with the funereal bees, this should not come as entirely unexpected]

the watchers say grimly to the diva, *you're clinging with your feet   get back to the story, centre screen*

ORCHIDS

When her handsome husband came in
the door with one big hand around
a green paper offering

power of magenta
pigment-shock

she was pleased, though they did not unlock
her heart. He'd brought orchids,
so bright they left
an afterimage on her retina.
She loved appearances that warmed.

cold hands
hard art

When he came in the door carrying the orchids high
— green paper shield —
she was preparing the communion
he had asked for:
dinner with candlelight.
The meal was savoury

earthy pleasures

when he walked in the door
and hot
with her, though she was ready
to flare at the least

scared, a windmill with the glint
of blue steel along each
whirling blade

wrong word.

Despite his orchids, they had another fight.
In the middle of the night, he got up
and went into the other room
to sleep.

Three days later, over breakfast,
she fell into the flowers' saturation.
It was like slipping into a pool.   rule of the bright wonderful
Instead of turquoise closing over her head
and the shimmer and undulation of light
on white concrete, it was magenta
and the glow of halogens suspended
over the table.   able, finally, to feel an efflorescence
                                                     of tenderness

He'd gone to work; wouldn't be back
for another four days.
They'd made up.
Now, when she looks at the orchids kindling
                                                     valid, the stuff you can handle
she wishes when he'd come in the door
she'd thrown her arms around him
and kissed his salty warm neck.
      She sees his face at the florist's
      picking them out: tired from work,
      anxious about coming home.
      I'll take these, he'd have said,
      holding out two bunches   lurch of the possible
      luminous as cages of tropical birds
      noisy in his worn hands.

Where is the calliope music? Where is home?

the cold velvet wheel?

Home again, I can groan, scratch, and talk to myself.
Mason Cooley

stellar mechanics onscreen

the woman asks, *why are plot points in real life so much harder to spot than on screen?*   the man makes a face, she swats him

    perspective: it's only when Death rides into town we can look back and judge the turning points

        [here the reader supplies the requisite empty black hood, the tall shambling horse, white for high contrast and ambiguity; perhaps this is the good guy]

so you're saying take the long view

    yeah

bright night view, out in the country with thousands of blazing pinpricks ricocheting down from a rubbed velvet sky?

    something like that, yeah

aww, you're my hero

Skeena River

Half a lifetime
of letting the Skeena flow   go
in and out her eyes
might still not be enough   the slow, textured mysteries
to take in its chill green language.

Along the shore,
ice is the shade of greyed sky.
Division of waters drawling
around islands. Flood plains   constrained
curve into hieroglyphs.

Cedars, cottonwoods with root balls
like scrotums, shrivelled and dried,
tweaked from the turning, muddy banks,
rush of air as the planet revolves.
Half a mile away on sandbars, tree bones
poke toward the horizon, beached
vertebra of marine mammals.

Magic winter,
the quick water alight with white
poured through wandering clouds.
Snuggled into the hill,   hesitate
a house with a tin roof waits;   *home* mystic as brushstrokes on a
                                        Chinese scroll

plume of smoke, cleared driveway.

She wants to stop,
go down, have this strange house
be home.

It faces the Skeena.

Surely, from its small warm rooms
the runes of water
would seep
clearly

banish fear, its obsessive wings
creak like a heron's

through her moving years.

FALLING IN LOVE (AGAIN)

What she wants you to understand
is the hypnotic nature   of sex
of trees; how they soothe

                                                    [speak for yourself!]

with green verticals.
Look at them: mountain after mountain
furred with long spikes, ragged
against the sky.   obvious symbolism
Trees make her feel
stilled.
She rips loose
from craving anything more.

                                                    wishful thinking a blue blanket
                                                    fleece with stars

In the mountains wolves, grizzlies,
black bears roam. They are the unknowns.
What's known you regret as if you'd toppled
every conifer yourself, are the ravages   in the beginning was sap-
                                                    sweet death
of logging.
Green says rest here,
says the silver *illuminati* of fallen trees
mixed with the living is just fine,

quit trying to remake   forsake
the garden of Eden.

TWO SHAPES

Who can endure such repetition?
Betrayal of the flesh   metaphor made flash
how it refuses to go any farther, stubborn
as a good dog when it sniffs a cougar, just sinks
to the trail and it's only when you shrug, turn
from the woods, the visual hit of green corduroy
in an unlit room, does it rise
again. Of course it's not until later
the cougar sighting's confirmed.

         but you'd guessed; why keep
         a dog and do your own barking?

Meanwhile the sun abandons the horizon.
Time to peruse one last paradigm
clear and lavender as the light left
when day falls behind
the mountains.

         hindbrain kicks into primate mode

All that remains after refusal
is pushing toward decency.
Domesticity a pillow. You're defended
with feathers. What a thrill.

         skill to get to your feet on
         the rushing board of blue
         adrenaline

The washing machine spins absolution;
on the green couch, the cat snores.

Behind the mountains loom more
mountains, ten thousand feet
with glaciers, icefields, the night terrors out hunting.
After dusk, you cower inside.
The drama plays out again:

this time will turn out different (you hope),
cherishing will whip you both into compliance.

Two shapes black and bent
as question marks   kiss   & miss
in the last ghostly bit
                    of violet
                              twilight.

PHYLLIS IN HOSPITAL

*I have come to believe over and over again that what is most important
to me must be spoken, made verbal and shared, even at the risk
of having it bruised or misunderstood.*
                    Audre Lorde

Think of these words as all the flowers
she ever grew:

armloads of gloriosa daisies,
the sweet bent-back tawny petals   *I read it to her,* her niece said. *I*
                                            don't know if she
                                            understood

in meadows.   Rain-wet lilacs to bury
a face in.   The white stars

of absence.   Lilies   struggled in a shade of things
                                            not said;
                                            sad-faced greyhound on a red
                                            leash

in her garden,

growing or not, you have no
way of knowing.

You loved her from the side-
lines all the fragrant long years   fifteen

of divorce. Her son shone
from the living room

in photographs when people dropped by
but you talked flowers   until it became audience
                                            and monologue

words rooted in the affection
women have for lost

members of families you can
claim only   obliquely.   dementia snapped on its chain

What you want her to know is this:
you and she are cuttings from a sprig

of tenderness, that like her, you adore   that last visit, to her
red lipstick   you were only a white shape passing,
          less than a pillowcase snapping
          clean
and courage, a kind of gallantry   on a line
that goes along with men

on horseback and walrus moustaches.
Like her husband, when she first met him

at the ranch.   The bustle and ruckus
of packing for up-coast.

Women in aprons buckling down
to the serious business of feast-making;   & didn't she excel?

salmon anointed with garlic and lemon, potato
salad and chocolate mousse for company.

Mornings, it is picnic weather, summer when sun
on cloudless mountains is the beginning of the world;

sea water around her island is green
and the *hish hish* of waves a friend beckoning her on
          diagnosed with cancer – it killed
          her father in twenty-one days –
          she turned
          her face to the wall, refused
          even water

adventures.   There are no bears on the beaches.
They are high

up the mainland slopes eating early berries   after
and in the garden at home

                                                          three

the clematis vine is studded with fat, lightly

                                                          weeks
perfumed buds about to open.

                                                          she —

TODAY THE GIANT COTTONWOOD

Today the giant cottonwood
says *Come here*. Its shape a raised-hand command
with blunt fingers snapped off;
wrist and forearm form the trunk,

you were in a funk, a spiky
purple squeeze ball

thicker than you are tall.

You go, grumbling:
what wisdom do cottonwoods have?
You worry about breakage;
maybe that's all cottonwoods know.
Off the path, through the salmonberry,
to balance on the mossy root
high as a desk.
The trunk at earth level had split
into crumbly brown.

admit it, this tree's been through
the lores [of wind]

Why should you believe anything
a cottonwood with a rotten heart says?
But you lean your forehead against its ridged bark,
peek to see you are hidden from the path
though your black dog crashes about in plain sight.

incite comment

The cottonwood shows *light in rings*.

You've seen this before, the hustle and shimmer
of orange, then dark, orange then…
The rings flicker like light on water.

The cottonwood shows *dark*.
Then light comes again, but slowly.
Light spins like a plate,
like Jupiter's rings, Neptune's.

What is the tree trying to say?   display, make tangible

Then a hole in your heart rips.
These are the cottonwood's *days*,
dark dark then light spreads out
the way a raindrop flattens on a convex surface:
at the centre is no-change.
Change, no-change.   range of motion

The hurt you'd come with drops
like cottonwood branches in a gale.
Who would have thought a cottonwood
would know so much   about movement?   alignment, the gentle grey

NORTH OF DEEP BAY

Home begins as fir trees

steam rises from soaked bark
in sun

get bigger, the yellowed energy
of cedars straightens.   Mountains reveal
curved blue testaments against the sky;
they are your own bones, gleaming.

Home is the wild coast, tempered
with gardens, with copper dahlias.
Scarlet runners flame up rough sticks.
Horses, so glossy you see the child
(grown or not) who stands beside them,
curry comb in hand, mouth full
of endearments.

clear this is *such*
a special velvet-nose

Home is the sea that rims the land
with susurrations of herons,
of gulls,
the wet red cling

brings contentment, rough & cold,
blown spume on the cheek

of Turkish towel seaweed, surprising in its hearth
shade – when old, it fades to pink.
The more conventional sheen of sea lettuce,
Kelly green.

Home is the sky clamped down
in a winter gale;
rain slips slantwise like blown smoke.   primacy of shelter
The deep clamour of branches
in the wind
and groaning with motion, the joy
of air that slides by, austere
and filled with secret
salt. Black surf scoters,
ridiculous with their hooked orange
bills.   *Fish ducks*   struck with sheer
                                                cartoon joy

you used to call them

Home is always firs,
their blackberry aroma
in sun; the piercing through of sweetness
a delight.   The eager snuffing along damp trails
after rain.
                                                again, the ringing-bell claim
                                                of land on imagination

          The first stars come out
          in a dusk sky;
          across it, fir shapes stamped inky black.   on track

          Silent reverberation of their needles.

HOME

Home is a place you are comfortable
with the smells: pell-mell of the snug
lemon furniture polish, the cold-air-
sweet smell of a dense-furred cat.
Home is a lift of the heart
at day's end, a place   space that rubs the right way,
                                                    your favourite sweater

you belong the way a jacket does
on a hook.

Home is the rub of just-washed sheets,
that anticipatory charge building:
soon, very soon, you will stop reading
get up and *do* something.
It's socks nesting in cupboards,
sneaking off with partners
of other pairs so you have
endless mismatches.
It's family who leave
trails through the house,
meteors flashing and streaking light
behind them, not to mention
laundry and the radio stations
they listen to, loudly,
which you don't like.
        And when it comes to stairs,   *think*: dance of the chairs
        your family has the subtlety
        of baby elephants.   blatant, adamant, the mechanical
                                                    clangour of a red bell buoy

Home is making food you know
they like: potato soup,
salads, cheese buns that fill
the house with that archetypal
yearning of bread baking.
Apple pie with whipped cream.
It's that smooth turn
of the wooden
spoon in gravy: *I will take over,*
now you.   construe this as glue

Home is the limp flag
of exhaustion by evening;
just when you've picked up your book
your daughter bounces
on the end of your bed
full of confidences
shiny and vivid as helium balloons.   purple, silver
Often you find the strength
to put down the book   look
and listen.

properties of light

stories of light generally lead the diva outside, that is   roofless, angling
toward some truth elusive as a cat that doesn't want to be caught   she
can't think properly until there's sky overhead

feeling at home is different from being home, though gleamy days exist
where she walks as though the two overlap and click to some slideways
dimension where the air is scented with fir or cottonwood and she
shimmies loose as an athlete ready for some shining endeavour   if she's
lucky there'll be the smell of moving water, clean and leaving behind a
particular freshness

light: noun
Middle English, from Old English *Eoht;* akin to Old High German *lioht*
light, Latin *luc-, lux* light, *lucEre* to shine, Greek *leukos* white

light travels at 186,281 miles per second
it makes vision possible: physical & metaphysical
light radiates, it's electromagnetic
divas gets high on light
bright is electromagnetic
bright travels at 300,00 k per second

does bright bend like a cat straightens itself in midair? or direct like some
stone Roman way down which her hero might trudge, unshaven, erotically
charged as a Marlboro Man   there's sideways sky, clean and no doubt
full of stories if a person were to speak the language of light, endorphins
perking, feeling in the world overhead, moving like a clean athlete, ready
for some fir or cottonwood at ease in a dimension which overlapping with
stimulation of the visual receptors such as a source of light, a celestial
body, or a particular illumination

CEDAR

Cedar's multiplicity of arms   *Shiva*, splintery
grow smaller toward the top
not like stacked starfish
but like sisters, hugging.
From beneath,
the drape of shelter,
welcome.
Yellow-green sleeves against the high
contrast blue of sky.   guarded, glowing
Cedar straightens itself   in the mind's home theatre,
                                                    we take these shapes with us

with determination toward
the nightly pull-past
of stars. It comforts them.

The sky slips by on a cold velvet wheel.
                                                    no sound, the soft revolve

Cedar is drawn towards the hard
dark of no atmosphere.
Cedar would hold its own
in the great fire codes of nebula
but it is rooted and defined
by lines of cellulose,
its aromatic shaggy bark,
and blackberries about its skirt,
say *You are of earth and dew and the ravens' perch.*

Gravity
pulls down cedar's fronds,
keeps them dandling the air.   beyond the unseen, the space
                                                    between, flips
                                                    to positive

Along its branches, cedar berries dangle
green as sunlit water in a cove.

Later in the season, ripened to brown,
cedar gifts its year's bounty
to the nightly tangle of white light at its tip,
                                        tribute

the bright lure.

WORKING UNTIL YOU'RE THE THINNESS OF AN IRONED SHIRT

You watch your poems startle
like starlings in a field
in autumn.   They cry, rush

                            brush by, dry & locked as feather
                            barbs, which link into
                            a continuous vane

toward the horizon with a *whoosh*,

lift over the bleached stubble of your life,
chatter energized, like they have some destination
they really want to be,
a generous non-spatial continuum

                            key & wilderness; there will be
                            mountains & rivers falling
                            down them, rejoicing & green

while you stay behind the power wires
which hem the cropland,
stitches arced black against pink sunset,
fields bereft of all but tunnelling voles
and knee-high shocks
of shorn corn.

                            you'd warn them but are too
                            jealous

Well, what can you say?
At best poems are flighty creatures.
At worst they lurk in kitchen drawers
sullen and pure as red-handled knives
that stab when you reach for them

                            condemn

though you would risk that now
to stroke again
one iridescent feather.

                            double drum: from both sides
                            of the separation,
                            the command *come*

MISTAKES HAVE A COLOUR

No one ever told you mistakes   an ache
have a colour, energy
motion, they're like low-flying comets,
not olive green or brown, none
of the basement-suite lurkers   berserk low lives

but white with pain, a sudden   burden to the neurons,
                                                 fundamental functional units

blow to the head, navy and starburst,
seeing the end of your life rush up,
oncoming car in your lane magnified,
slow motion.
You anticipate the opening
of a tunnel, isn't that how the narrative goes,
what finds us afterward?   onboard & golden

You swing from this anticipation
like a maypole drenched in unreasonable rain,

foliage hanging loose, mock orange
sending out a message
of citrus into damp air *return to sender*
address you can no longer find symbols for;
the black cursive is there but meaning unknown

for as you quarrel with the present
resistance and crumpling metal catapult
you toward the future at supersonic   diatonic
speed, the maypole half a continent away now.

You still clutch soaked pink ribbons in your hands,
the white insistence of fragrance long gone. withdrawn from the bank
                                              of *all will be well*

White is the exact shade of mistake.

THE TRIANGLE NO-NOSE OF A SKULL

Remember when you were in love
and all the primary brights sizzled
on your retina, dove
deep into nimbleness;
flash of merry-go-round horses

                                  force of longing the central
                                  steel pin

coursing white, red and gilt?

Remember the innocence of wet hair?
Secrets silt-hued as bare jawbones
Iroquois skulls in a museum
case when you were four; the gleam
of glass, and behind it real teeth?

                                  beneath

You emerged fascinated with the triangle
no-nose of death, the closed
griefs we rise from;
you leave now, climb
from a pool into August afternoon
blue as molten sapphire

                                  fire & it's as though
                                  you manage to walk away
                                  with only second-degree burns

though your staggered heart says *impossible*.

Love is a fossil.   apostle of melted metal
Like death, it is sudden and permanent,
bequeaths calcium, the memory of breath;
who and what we love marks us, right in the bone.

Striations of guilt and anger, danger:
there is no exhilaration like the direct gaze
of the beloved; you recall, flush
with a rush of shame.

Wrong life for that one.   but what was begun is gone

Remember to tell bones that before the sound
of calliope music, your painted horse rising
dream-like, skin scintillating with water
as you climb the pool's white steps.   scold

Remember as your feet touch
warm red brick that you are willing
to be satisfied, to be brown and loving

with a nose in August.   presuppose only the tangible

fast-forward

in the movie, the h. hero exchanges looks with the diva that are hotter
than a burning fireplace in a kitchen —

[the hero returned once the diva finished her solo]

— think oven on, spareribs baking in rich barbeque sauce, the fireplace
performing its decorative flicker of flame, the soothing story of home-
will-make-everything-all-right — if you doubt this, try being sick away
from home   the protagonists are at a feast in the great hall   multiple
wolfhounds hover/hoover, but later, as the diva and the hero embrace
beside a canopied bed, the same messenger who'd arrived with news of
the inciting incident interrupts them   there's an invasion

and at the second-act turning point, the hero rides off with death into the
bright darks of sunset, the diva has to save the kingdom   an elderly
shaman with a Fu Manchu moustache appears as a mentor

after the climactic battle, the forces of fangs and no fashion sense routed,
it's summer, midmorning, the diva is mounted on a shining black horse
[every inch a male] cantering up the hill to the palace, loving every minute
of the cheers, attention, her amazing costume arc-light white   wing-
sleeves flash like metaphors repeating in the light

she confides to her horse, *on my earlier solo the hero said, "sing so low they can't*
hear you." I clouted him but good with his own scarlet varlet expectations   I haven't
any intention — ever — of slipping from centre stage

from the bed, the watchers laugh   *right on,* the woman says   *I guess*
none of us expects to die   the man scratches his nose, thinks I'm not going
to die, at least not now or next week

Einstein's cat [very very long], says zip but is ready to do something
wicked about that NY to LA tail-pull, for after all, *it* belongs at the story's
relative
                              centre

ACKNOWLEDGEMENTS

Thanks to the editors of the following books and magazines who
published poems in this book.

Canadian Literature: "Lethe," "Phyllis in Hospital"
Elements of English 11 (Nelson): "Polaris"
Event: "Baby Stars: South Pender Island," "Star Charts"
The Fiddlehead: "Milky Way," "Falling in Love (Again)," "April Ghosts"
NeWest Review: "Cedar"
Room: "Face Down in a Field of Stars," "Polaris," "At Some Level of the
          Universe," "Trust and Poppies"
Prairie Fire: "March is a Lit Month"
Prism International: "North of Deep Bay"
Quarter Moon Quarterly: "Cedar"
The Prairie Journal of Canadian Literature: "Star Blood"
The Malahat Review: "When He Left, the Air Smelled Like Cold Water and
          Stone"
The New Orphic Review: "Skeena River"
The Saranac Review (US): "The Triangle No-Nose of a Skull"
The West Coast Fisherman: "Skeena River"
The Windsor Review: "Wake with Candles," "Home"

The spine of poems in the book that forms the sequence of *Einstein's Cat*
was shortlisted for the 2008 CBC Awards.

Zoë Landale's writing has appeared in over thirty anthologies and her fiction, creative nonfiction and poetry has won significant awards, including first prize for poetry in the CBC Literary Competition. *Einstein's Cat* is her seventh book. She also edited, with Luanne Armstrong, *Slice Me Some Truth: An anthology of Canadian creative nonfiction*, which was published by Wolsak and Wynn in 2011. Her work has appeared in numerous literary journals and magazines including *The New Quarterly*, *CV2*, *The Antigonish Review*, *The Malahat Review*, *Chatelaine* and *Canadian Living*. She is a member of the Writer's Union of Canada and the Federation of BC Writers. Landale lives in British Columbia where she is a faculty member of the Creative Writing Department at Kwantlen Polytechnic University.